I0884727

God's Perfect Will

God's Perfect Will

BY

Rev. G. CAMPBELL MORGAN

AUTHOR OF
"GOD'S METHODS WITH MAN," "LIFE PROBLEMS,"
"WHEREIN HAVE WE ROBBED GOD?" "THE
SPIRIT OF GOD," ETC., ETC.

Wipf & Stock
PUBLISHERS
Eugene, Oregon

Wipf and Stock Publishers
199 W 8th Ave, Suite 3
Eugene, OR 97401

God's Perfect Will
By Morgan, G. Campbell
ISBN: 1-59244-801-1
Publication date 8/23/2004
Previously published by Fleming H. Revell Company, 1901

A notice to the reader: this reproduction is an exact facsimile of the 1901, Fleming Revell edition. The reader should note that pages 105 to 112 and pages 123 to 124 are missing from the pagination of the original, but does not indicate any missing text from the book.

To

MY FOUR CHURCHES

Stone

Rugeley

Birmingham: Westminster Road

London: New Court

All of which have in varied ways contributed to the making of the ministry which has endeavoured to express some of the music which lies within the inexhaustible theme of

GOD'S PERFECT WILL

For their patience, their help, their affection, I shall thank God—if I rightly understand the unseen things—for ever

G. CAMPBELL MORGAN

"Epaphras, who is one of you, a servant of Christ Jesus, saluteth you, always striving for you in his prayers, that ye may stand perfect and fully assured in all the will of God."

COLOSSIANS iv. 12.

Contents

The Supreme Subject

"I worship Thee, sweet Will of God!
And all Thy ways adore;
And every day I live, I seem
To love Thee more and more.

. . . . . .

"Man's weakness, waiting upon God,
Its end can never miss,
For men on earth no work can do
More angel-like than this.

"Ride on, ride on triumphantly,
Thou glorious Will, ride on!
Faith's pilgrim sons behind Thee take
The road that Thou hast gone.

"He always wins who sides with God,
To him no chance is lost;
God's Will is sweetest to him when
It triumphs at his cost.

"Ill, that He blesses, is our good,
And unblest good is ill;
And all is right that seems most wrong,
If it be His sweet Will."

F. W. Faber.

GOD'S PERFECT WILL

PROLOGUE

THE SUPREME SUBJECT

THERE is no phrase more often in use in Christian thought and speech than that of "The Will of God." It constantly recurs in our reading of Scripture; our hymns are very many of them concerned with it; and in prayer we give utterance to it again and again.

This familiarity has in some measure robbed us of a keen sense of its vital importance. Its meaning is all too little realized. In common with many of the most sacred things, it has largely become a kind of fetish that is worshipped because it has a sound of piety; while the fact that it is the supreme subject of revelation, and the one and only abiding law of life, is forgotten. Notions that are false in themselves, and, therefore, pernicious in their effects, are held concerning it. These are not the result of thought, but rather of the lack of thought. There are many who imagine that the Will of God is something apart from human interests, to which men are to be resigned whenever they happen to be brought into contact with it. Frances Ridley Havergal said that "there is always a sigh of regret in resignation." This is perfectly true; and that conception of the Will of God which looks upon it as a Divine interference to which we are to be resigned, is evil in its effects. How many there are who only think of their relation to the Will of God in times of sorrow and trial. They are perfectly sincere, therefore, when they sing—

> " If Thou shouldst call me to resign
> What most I prized—it ne'er was mine;
> I only yield Thee what was Thine:
> Thy will be done!"

Yet the very words of the hymn reveal the fact that the singer does not truly understand the safety, the blessedness, the delight of dwelling in the circle of the Divine Will.

The one and only law of life that sets a man free from all the forces that blight and destroy is the Will of God. Show me a man who lives for one day wholly, utterly, in word and thought and deed in the Will of God, and I will show you a man who is antedating heaven, and who for that day reaches the plane of life which is at once broadest, freest, and gladdest.

God's Perfect Will

The word of God is given to man not that he may have a correct *theory,* but that he may have the truth. Truth is a sanctifying force, and a man holds the truth only when he is held by the truth. When truth possesses a man, all its glory and beauty are manifested through his life and character. The truth the Bible reveals is the Will of God for man. Sanctification by truth is the bringing of man into the Will of God.

"The means of grace" are means to an end, that end being the realization of the Will of God. Every one of them tends to that issue.

"The hope of glory" is the hope that ultimately the Will of God will be done upon the earth as in the heaven, or that the spirit of man, passing into the heavenly state, shall realize all the full blessedness of that Will.

All prayer lies within the two petitions of the pattern prayer the Master taught His disciples: "Thy kingdom come; Thy will be done." There is no prayer beyond that. It may be divided into sentences and syllables, and made to fit the necessity of the hour; but when prayer moves the heart of God, it is because it is confined within that compass.

Allow your imagination to carry you back to the past ages. Amid the silences of that immeasurable eternity you are conscious of perfect peace, perfect happiness, perfect love. The explanation is to be found in the fact that the Will of God was perfectly done. None can declare the genesis of evil, but its nature is clearly known—it is rebellion against the Will of God. The mystery of how that first came to be, is absolutely inscrutable, but the fact is established beyond question.

God's Perfect Will

We are but infinitesimal portions of the universe of God, but the being of the smallest particle of created things is conditioned in His Will, and its success or failure depends upon its realization of, or failure to realize, that Will. The supreme subject in every life, then, is that His Will should be discovered and obeyed.

To-day we are hearing much on every hand on such subjects as the filling of the Spirit, holiness, power for service. This is cause for gratitude; but, after all, these are means to an end, and that end is the Will of God. A Spirit-filled man is a most glorious being; but by that condition he has not reached the goal, he has only become equipped for fulfilling the essential of his life. Holiness is to be sought and found. A holy man is not, however, to rest in his holiness. It is health for perpetual obedience. Power for service is a great blessing, but service as response to the Will of God is the supreme matter.

The most vital consideration for every human life is as to whether we are, and do, that which accords with the Will of God.

John declares (1 John ii. 17) that the doing of the Will of God is the condition of permanence amid the perishing and passing of the world. We are conscious that all around is perishing; yea, and we ourselves, as to bodily powers, pass away. We are also conscious of a passionate desire for permanence. The possessive pronouns are at once a revelation of that desire, and a confession of weakness. "My house"; and it is gone! "My child";

and it is dead! There is permanence only in the Will of God, and there only can we fully use the possessive pronoun, " My Lord and my God."

The Message of the Old Testament

"When people read, 'The law came by Moses, but grace and truth by Christ,' do they suppose it means that the law was ungracious and untrue? The law was given for a foundation; the grace (or mercy) and truth for fulfilment;—the whole forming one glorious Trinity of judgment, mercy, and truth. And if people would but read the text of their Bibles with heartier purpose of understanding it, instead of superstitiously, they would see that throughout the parts which they are intended to make most personally their own (the Psalms), it is always the Law which is spoken of with chief joy. The Psalms respecting mercy are often sorrowful, as in thought of what it cost; but those respecting the law are always full of delight. David cannot contain himself for joy in thinking of it—he is never weary of its praise:—'How love I Thy law! it is my meditation all the day. Thy testimonies are my delight and my counsellors; sweeter, also, than honey and the honeycomb.'"

RUSKIN ("Modern Painters").

THE MESSAGE OF THE OLD TESTAMENT

I

THE Old Testament declares the beginnings of created things, and gives us the history of the race from Creation to four hundred years prior to the coming of Christ. The underlying current of truth running through all its pages has tc do with the one subject of the Will of God. Let the panorama of life move before the eye of the mind. Note well its darkness and light, its places of agony and of rapture. Mark the deeds which appal, and the heroisms which thrill. From beginning to end, the character of the picture is determined by the relation of men or nations to the Will of God. This is the great message of the Old Testament, that all the rivers that have made sad the life of man have had their source in his departure from that "good and perfect and acceptable Will of God"; and all the streams that have made glad the probationary pilgrimage of individuals, or the cities wherein men have dwelt, have sprung from the throne of God, which is the seat of His government.

The historical books tell the story of the wandering of man from God again and again, and show how all such wandering issued in disaster. They also reveal the one unending purpose of God to bring man back into harmony with that Will. The methods were many; the intention one. The devout of all the ages breathed, if not in words yet in spirit, the same prayer—"Thy kingdom come; Thy will be done." The very essence of evil lay in the rebellion of the human heart against that Kingdom and that Will.

The devotional books are all occupied with the same theme. The songs find their keynote in the kinghood and throne of God. "The Lord reigneth." "Thy throne, O God, is for ever and ever." These and kindred phrases tell the character of the music. When the song is of human experience at its best, it is ever of the joy and peace to be found in the law of God. "Oh how I love Thy law." "Thy commandment is exceeding broad." When the music becomes a dirge, it is because in individual or national life God has been forgotten. "When I kept silence my bones waxed old through my roaring." "The fool hath said in his heart, There is no

God." Or, if you read aright the prayers, they are all part and parcel of the aspiration of man, after a realization of the Divine purpose and pathway. "Teach me to do Thy will, O God." "Make haste to help me, O Lord, my salvation."

The prophetic books have a like significance. The burden that oppressed these men, until they delivered themselves in words of flaming fire, was a burden of Divine judgment and government. Nations that had forgotten God were called back to allegiance. Nations persisting in their waywardness were told of their doom. The perpetual cry of the prophets was, "Let the wicked forsake his way, and the unrighteous man his thoughts, and let him return to the Lord." These men spake as the oracles of God, without fear or faltering, and their message was ever a "Thus saith the Lord"; and the secret of their daring and devotion the fact that each could say, "The Lord, before Whom I stand."

Or if we take another method of considering the message of the Old Testament, we shall arrive at the same result. Range before your vision all the hosts of the men of all the centuries. They stand now in imagination like a long chain of hills stretching far back to the first man Adam—"which was the son of God." Such an outlook at once reveals certain men that stand out from among their fellows, their heads raised above them, capped with the pure snows, and catching first and keeping last the light of the sun. Adam, Abel, Enoch, Noah, Abraham, Moses, David, Elijah, and others that space forbids our naming. What makes the difference between these and their fellows? In every case the measure of their superiority is the measure of their understanding of, and obedience to, the Will of God.

Adam erect, is so because he fulfils the purpose of God. Abel received, is so because he lives a life God-centred rather than self-centred. Enoch's distinction is revealed in his brief biography, "Enoch walked with God." Noah, also, amid the most appalling corruption, believed God, and was saved in the works of obedience that grew out of his faith. Abraham became the father of the faithful because he went out, not knowing whither he went, confident alone in the wisdom and rightness of the word of God. Moses, having himself learned to wait for the guidance of God, gave the world a code of ethics which remains the foundation of morality to this day, because it was first written with the finger of God. David's memory is revered more for his harp than his crown, and that because, through it, he sang of the law of his God. Elijah still stands as the type of rough, magnificent character, because he was the messenger of law to an apostate age. These were all great, inasmuch as they abode in the Will of God; and the things that smirch the escutcheon of each, were of the nature of disobedience or wandering from the Divinely-marked pathway.

Thus, from the song of new-born earth to the fiery warning of Malachi, the Old Testament brings us face to face with the supreme subject.

The Message of the New Testament

"Thou wert the end, the blessèd rule
Of Jesu's toils and tears;
Thou wert the passion of His heart,
Those three-and-thirty years."

F. W. Faber.

THE MESSAGE OF THE NEW TESTAMENT

II

If the Old Testament is occupied with the Will of God as its supreme subject, the New Testament is in all its parts an unveiling and exposition thereof, both as to nature and possibility.

For the purpose of a general survey, we shall divide the New Testament into its three principal sections of historic, didactic, and prophetic books. These include—

1. *Historic.* The Gospels and Acts.
2. *Didactic.* The Epistles.
3. *Prophetic.* The Revelation.

In the first we have the story of the life

of Jesus, and the first chapter in His larger life resulting from the work He accomplished. Also His teaching, containing unified truth, which became clear in the subsequent light of the Spirit's teaching.

In the second we have the unfolding of truth for the individual believer and the Church, by men indwelt and inspired by the Holy Spirit.

In the third we have, for the most part, visions of the closing scenes of the present dispensation and the accomplishment of Divine purposes through Divine power.

In all of these the subject is the Will of God.

The life of Jesus realized it, and His teaching declared its nature and necessity. The men whose doings are recorded in the Acts lived wholly in, and only for, that Will. The consummation of all is the triumph of righteousness and love by the complete submission of humanity thereto.

I. *Historic.*

Taking these in the order named, we come first to the historic books. The roots of the New are in the Old. We therefore go back to the Psalms for the keynote of these books. " Sacrifice and offering Thou hast no delight in; mine ears hast Thou opened: burnt offering and sin offering hast Thou not required. Then said I, Lo, I am come; in the roll of the book it is written of me: I delight to do *Thy will,* O my God." None will deny that this belongs to the New Testament, for we are agreed that these words had their perfect fulfilment in the person and experience of Jesus.

God's Perfect Will

Underlying everything in the fourfold Gospel of Matthew, Mark, Luke, and John is the perpetual sounding of this note of perfect music, "I delight to do Thy will, O my God." In the life of Jesus it was the reason for all He did, and the inspiration of all He said. Whether living as a boy in His mother's home, or working as a man at His trade of carpenter; whether going to the Jordan for baptism, or to the wilderness for temptation; whether preaching to the crowds, or working wonders of love among the needy—His life was perpetually filled with delight in the Will of God. Once only in the history of the human race has there been a life true to the Divine ideal. That was the life of Jesus.

When His mother found Him in the Temple, He said to her, "Wist ye not that I must be in My Father's house?"

(Luke ii. 49). His Father's Will for Him was that He should be a disciple among the teachers of His people, and that was the explanation of His tarrying behind at Jerusalem.

When He faced and overcame temptation, He did so in the strength of the fact that "Man shall not live by bread alone, but by every word that proceedeth out of the mouth of God" (Matt. iv. 4). And when His disciples urged Him upon one occasion to eat, He replied, "My meat is to do the will of Him that sent Me, and to accomplish His work" (John iv. 34). He needed bread; but the supreme necessity was that He should do the Will of God. That was the sustenance of His deepest life. In reply to the criticisms of His enemies, He dared to say, "He that sent Me is with Me; He hath not left Me alone; for I do always the things that are pleasing to Him" (John viii. 29).

The Will of God was equally the sum and substance of His teaching. Indeed, it is impossible to separate between His teaching and Himself. He said, "I *am* the Truth," not "I teach the truth." When I see what He is, I know what He is going to teach me; and when I hear what He teaches, I know what He is.

His Sermon on the Mount is the Magna Charta of the Will of God, the most wonderful words that ever fell on the ears of man.

"Happy!" (Matt. v. 3). That is the first of them, and it is the keynote of all that follows, declaring immediately what is the Will of God for man. In solemn words He sets the doing of that Will at the very wicket of the kingdom, not as pass-word—there are no words that will pass men into heaven's kingdom—but as the condition upon which men may enter: "Not every one that saith unto Me, Lord, Lord, shall enter into the kingdom of heaven; but he that doeth the will of My Father which is in heaven" (Matt. vii. 21); and closes with that most wonderful claim for Himself, "Every one, therefore, which heareth these words of Mine, and doeth them, shall be likened unto a wise man, which built his house upon the rock" (Matt. vii. 24).

Thus the Gospels unveil the perfect ideal in life and teaching of the man who does the Will of God.

The Acts of the Apostles opens with the significant words, "The former treatise I made, O Theophilus, concerning all that Jesus began both to do and to teach" (Acts i. 1). The reference Luke makes to a "former treatise" is of course to his Gospel, and he declares that Gospel to be the story of beginnings only. The inference is that the second treatise is a story of continuation; and this we discover to be so as we read, for the history is one of the doing of the Will of God by Spirit-filled men. What men they were! They moved the world! Study that wonderful fifth chapter. What a state the priests were in! Nothing so troubles the priest as to come in contact with men doing the Will of God. They said to Peter and the rest, "We straitly charged you not to teach in this name: and behold, ye have filled Jerusalem with your teaching" (Acts v. 28). There is no finer testimony to apostolic work on record. A mere handful of men had filled Jerusalem with their teaching, and it was teaching that gripped, for the priests continued—"and intend to bring this Man's blood upon us" (Acts v. 28).

In Peter's answer, in a brief sentence he reveals the secret of these phenomena that so perplexed and baffled the priests, "*We must obey God!*" (Acts v. 29). That is the secret. These men shook kingdoms to their foundations and turned the world upside down, their enemies being witness; and the reason of their success lay in their abandonment to the Will of God.

II. *Didactic.*

Turning to the didactic writings, we find the same great theme in all. Take illustrations from the writings of Peter, James, and John.

1. PETER. "Forasmuch then as Christ suffered in the flesh, arm ye yourselves also with the same mind; for he that

hath suffered in the flesh hath ceased from sin; that ye no longer should live the rest of your time in the flesh to the lusts of men, but to *the will of God*" (1 Pet. iv. 1, 2). That is Peter's conception of the meaning of the Christ-life.

2. JAMES. "*Go* to now, ye that say, To-day or to-morrow we will go into this city, and spend a year there, and trade, and get gain: whereas ye know not what shall be on the morrow. What is your life? For ye are a vapour, that appeareth for a little time, and then vanisheth away. For that ye ought to say, *If the Lord will,* we shall both live, and do this or that" (James iv. 13-15). James does not deny that we have to make arrangements for to-day and to-morrow. He insists that concerning them all we should say, "If the Lord will."

3. JOHN. "The world passeth away,

and the lust thereof: but he that *doeth the will of God* abideth for ever" (1 John ii. 17). John declares the Will of God to be the place of permanence, and all outside that Will is doomed to perish.

From these turn to the Pauline letters, and still the theme is the same: "I beseech you therefore, brethren, by the mercies of God, to present your bodies a living sacrifice, holy, acceptable to God, which is your reasonable service. And be not fashioned according to this world: but be ye transformed by the renewing of your mind, that ye may prove what is the *good and acceptable and perfect will of God*" (Rom. xii. 1, 2). The apostle's object in calling us to surrender ourselves is that we may prove the goodness, acceptability, and perfectness of the Will of God.

"For this cause we also, since the day

we heard it, do not cease to pray and make request for you, that ye may be filled with the *knowledge of His will* in all spiritual wisdom and understanding" (Col. i. 9). That is the burden of his prayer—not for Colossian believers only, but also for all those in whom he was interested.

The distinctive glory of the letter to the Hebrews is that it deals with the bringing in of "better things" which shall make men "perfect in every good thing *to do His will*" (Heb. xiii. 21).

Jude looks forward in his doxology to that day in which the Church shall be presented "before the presence of His glory without blemish in exceeding joy" (Jude 24).

All these writers agree, that the Will of God fulfilled in human life is the purpose of Christ in His people, and through His people in the world.

III. *Prophetic.*

Lastly, we turn to the prophetic book of the Revelation. Of this there are many interpretations, but there are points of perfect agreement. To one of these we now come. "And the four and twenty elders and the four living creatures fell down and worshipped God that sitteth on the throne, saying, Amen; Hallelujah. And a voice came forth from the throne, saying, Give praise to our God, all ye His servants, ye that fear Him, the small and the great. And I heard as it were the voice of a great multitude, and as the voice of many waters, and as the voice of mighty thunders, saying, Hallelujah; for the Lord our God, the Almighty, reigneth" (Rev. xix. 4-6). Differences of opinion exist as to the methods by which that glorious consummation is to be reached, but we all believe the time is coming when the Lord God Omnipotent shall reign and His Will be done. "Amen; Hallelujah." These words reveal the source of the blessedness of that glad day. God on the throne, and humanity saying "Amen" in consent, and "Hallelujah" in praise.

We commenced this study in the Psalms. Let us return there for a moment in conclusion. "Save us, O Lord our God, and gather us from among the nations, to give thanks unto Thy holy name, and to triumph in Thy praise. Blessed be the Lord, the God of Israel, from everlasting even to everlasting: and let all the people say, Amen, Hallelujah" (Ps. cvi. 47, 48, *margin*). Now read again the song of the Apocalypse, " And the four and twenty elders and the four living creatures fell down and worshipped God that sitteth on the throne, saying, Amen; Hallelujah" (Rev. xix. 4). Ransomed and redeemed humanity saying " Amen "—so be it, to the Will of God; and after the Amen, " Hallelujah "—praise the Lord.

That is the consummation. The Old prays for it; the New predicts and prepares for it. We may dream dreams of its splendour, but no dream can compass the reality, it is too great. Humanity, in every beating pulse, every fibre of its being, every drawing breath, saying " Amen " to the Will of God, " Hallelujah " to His government.

Thus Old and New, the one Bible, declares that the Divine Will is the only law of human life that satisfies the heart of God and ensures the well-being of man.

This very fact is that which gives supreme importance to Holy Scripture, and should condition all attempts to study it. There is, undoubtedly, room for devout criticism, study of the question of dates, and authorship; and there should ever be the widest toleration for different interpretations of many of the mysteries dealt with, which are, after all, beyond the possibility of full and final statement. To treat the Bible, however, as literature merely, or to read it with a view to formulating certain systems of belief, is to fail to realize its highest value, or to touch its deepest significance.

On its every page there is unfolded something of the Divine order, method, and purpose in the government of man. While the chronicles reveal the fault and failures of sinning men, all through there moves the Spirit of God, revealing the fact of His Kingship; and in every message of Psalmist, Seer, or Prophet, there is the unmistakable call to loyalty and obedience.

It is only as this is remembered, and the study of the Book is approached with sincere desire to discover the purpose of God in human life, and the laws which make that purpose possible of realization, that the Book answers its highest intention.

A Threefold Demand

"The steps of the way I know not,
But my Leader I know full well;
My hand is in His, I fear not—
In the depths of His peace I dwell.
He knows where He leads; I know not,
But I trust in His love each day:
My heart is His own; I fear not,
For the way is my Lord's highway.

"The hours may seem dark and dreary,
But His presence my life shall cheer;
The night may seem sad and weary,
But I know that my Lord is near.
One step at a time He shows me,
And I know that the rest He hides,
That love may the better show me
How in safety His mercy guides.

"I wait, in His will abiding;
I rejoice, for His strength sustains;
I trust in His word confiding;
And of doubt not one trace remains.
And never comes pain or sadness
But to hasten the sunlit morn;
Then grief shall give way to gladness,
Then never a sigh be born."

E. G. Wellesley-Wesley
("Songs of the Heart").

A THREEFOLD DEMAND

III

In our previous studies we have seen that the supreme subject of Scripture is the Will of God. As a revelation to man, it declares that human life is only perfectly conditioned as it discovers that Will, and yields implicit obedience thereto. In the present study we shall ask certain questions from the standpoint of conscious human need. Let it be granted that law in some form is a necessity; that anarchy of individual or social being is chaos and confusion; the question at once arises as to the highest and best law possible. A rough-and-ready division of the mass of men to-day will reveal three classes.

First, there are those who are the slaves of others. Human opinion is the test of all their doing and speaking. Conventionality holds them in an iron grip. They will do, or refuse to do, anything according to the opinion of some one else. The habit of the crowd becomes the rule of life. Or it may be that some one person is looked to as lawgiver; that person being sometimes called priest, at others teacher. The craving is for authority outside one's own personality; and this is sought in many ways.

Then there are those who affect to despise the opinion of others, and are openly and avowedly self-confident. They care not what others do, they are capable of making their own programme, conducting their own affairs. These are the people who make time-tables for themselves and form resolutions and surround themselves with a whole system of self-created safety laws.

Lastly, there are those who decline to be governed by the opinion of others, and who have absolutely abandoned attempting to control themselves by self-made programmes and regulations, and whose whole lives are conditioned in the prayer of the Psalmist of old: "Teach me to do Thy Will; for Thou art my God" (Psa. cxliii. 10).

The test as to which of these is really the highest law of life is to be found within the consciousness of man himself. There are certain aspirations of the human heart which are ever present. They may be distorted or dwarfed, but in some form they abide as the necessary and unalterable desires of human nature. The law of life which realizes and satisfies these, to the fullest possible extent, must of necessity be the best. These aspirations may be summarized under three heads—Perfection, Pleasure, Perpetuity.

I. *Perfection.*

The first aspiration of every human life is for Perfection. How strange and inexplicable, by the way, is the fear some excellent people have of the word. With what bated breath, and what aloofness of fear, is one often asked if one really believes in Christian perfection. And yet what else can one believe in who believes in Christ? Try other phrases—Christian imperfection, for instance. Will not some one explain that for us? Or. if you prefer, take another form of the negative—imperfect Christianity. Alas, yes, there is much of it; but who will say they believe in it? Let us have done with this unholy fear of a phrase, and at once say that nothing can satisfy the deepest demand of our human nature except its perfection. It is the common passion of the race, often partially realized and constantly abused, but perpetually present.

Who is there that would not immediately secure physical perfection if that were possible? To be vigorous, proportioned, and beautiful, would be a blessing no sane person would despise. Mental perfection is much less coveted because harder to attain, yet none would refuse to make some effort to attain it if it were within measurable distance. Spiritual perfection is alas most neglected, probably because it moves on the highest plane; yet no person, upon calm reflection. would deliberately reject this if they were once convinced of its accessibility.

This, then, is the first demand by which we propose to test any law or philosophy of life. It must be of such a nature as to ensure the ultimate perfection of our being, not on one side merely, but in its tripartite character of spirit, soul, and body.

II. *Pleasure.*

The second demand is for Pleasure. This is a perfectly legitimate demand, because it comes out of the deepest necessities of human nature, and is common to men everywhere, under most diversified conditions of life. In all ages, in all lands, and under all circumstances of life, man desires and seeks after happiness. It is very doubtful if a single exception can be found to this rule in the ranks of the human family. We occasionally hear of such a thing as misanthropy; and some there are who even venture to affirm that they have seen a misanthrope. Some of us have never had such a sorrowful experience, thank God!

There are men who seem to have no fellowship with the ordinary pursuits of pleasure, and are devoid of humor of a certain kind; but it has been discovered often that in some hidden and least expected place they have had their treasure-house of happiness. That it was not of the nature of the things that make other men happy does not matter for a moment. Even if it be granted that there are some human beings who are all that is intended by the word misanthrope, the true facts of their condition are quaintly revealed in the saying that they are only happy when miserable, for out of their discontent they are attempting to minister to the universal craving for pleasure.

Man was not made for sorrow. It is, we believe, a Divine ministrant of blessing, and in many cases precedes gladness; but the transient character of sorrow in the purpose of God is marked by the glorious promise that He will wipe all tears away. The heart of man was made for peace, and joy, and love; and through all the foolish blundering of popular pleasure-seeking, it is after these men seek.

By this also, therefore, we test the laws of life that are proposed to us. They must secure for us the highest and fullest pleasure; not that which is unsubstantial and evanescent, but the deep and the abiding; and the law which most perfectly does this is the best, and to it we will yield our wholehearted allegiance.

III. *Perpetuity.*

The last demand is that of Perpetuity. Man is everywhere, and at all times, and in every way, at war with decay. The hatred of death, and the loathing of the grave, mark the fact that man has capacity for life, and therefore feels rebellious against the faintest suggestion of its cessation.

How men strive after perpetuity! The search of old for the elixir of life was a pathetic proof of this craving; and in cases where men have been unable to hope for actual continuity of being, they have sought to perpetuate their existence in the memory of others by writings and works, and even by monuments erected.

We cry out for the beyond. Horizons are always a menace to our peace. We crave the infinite. Deeply conscious of the perishing nature of everything around us; seeing the dark sentence, "passing away," writ large upon our most valued treasures, and feeling ourselves ceaselessly moving through the pages of our life's story to the dreaded word FINIS—we sigh, and sob, and fret, and demand some place that passes not; some treasure that vanishes not away; some secret of being that will enable us to say, We abide, masters of death.

True it is, that thousands of us seem to float easily through the days, unconscious of these cravings, content to drift and not to know. Yet this is but false seeming. Carefully observe the first ordinary, every-day, matter-of-fact man in any crowd in any city, in any land. Keep close to him, that you may watch him. Presently, in a moment of loneliness, when the things unseen come near in overwhelming reality, or when he faces death and feels it imminent, or when some cherished hope is suddenly blighted, that man will lift his eyes and gaze wistfully toward the future. In those eyes shine the light of his true being, and the passion for perpetuity is revealed as being the true and perpetual sub-consciousness of his life.

That law of life which could answer that demand, and make man master of all the forces of disintegration and decay, is assuredly the highest and the best; and when we find it, to it we will abandon ourselves with whole-hearted devotion.

Thus standing within the realm of my own being, turning a deaf ear for the moment to all the babel of outside voices, I hear the speech of my true life, and learn its deepest demands; and I solemnly, deliberately, and positively declare that if the Will of God for man be, as the Bible declares it to be, the highest philosophy of human life, it must meet this threefold demand, and secure to me the perfection of my being, the highest and abiding pleasure, and that victory over the elements of death and decay which shall ensure my perpetuity.

In three subsequent chapters we shall endeavour to show that this is exactly what the Will of God does, and what any other law of life fails to do. In concluding the present study, it will be sufficient to summarize the subjects of the next three thus:

1. God's Will is perfect, because by Him man was created, and He therefore is alone able to make such laws as shall ensure man's perfection.

2. God's Will is perfect, because He is love, and Love only can make laws for man which will provide him with perfect pleasure.
3. God's Will is perfect, because He *is*, and the Eternal alone can make laws which take in all the past, present, and future, so as to secure perpetuity.

Provides Perfection

"Strong Son of God, immortal Love,
Whom we, who have not seen Thy face,
By faith, and faith alone, embrace,
Believing where we cannot prove.

"Thine are these orbs of light and shade;
Thou madest Life in man and brute;
Thou madest Death: and lo, Thy foot
Is on the skull which Thou hast made.

"Thou wilt not leave us in the dust:
Thou madest man, he knows not why,
He thinks he was not made to die;
And Thou hast made him: Thou art just.

"Thou seemest human and divine,
The highest, holiest manhood, Thou;
Our wills are ours, we know not how;
Our wills are ours, to make them Thine."

TENNYSON ("In Memoriam").

PROVIDES PERFECTION

IV

In considering the threefold demand dealt with in the last chapter, we come first in order to the demand for perfection. The answer of the Will of God to that demand may be briefly stated.

> God's Will is perfect, because by Him man was created, and He, therefore, is alone able to make such laws as shall ensure man's perfection.

This is coming down to a statement of the simplest kind. We all profess to believe that God has given us our being, and in a deep conviction of that truth lies the reason why we should yield ourselves wholly to His government in order that we may attain perfection of being.

Perhaps it is necessary to emphasize this initial fact, for oftentimes the teacher's greatest difficulty is to get men to accept the truth of the truth they accept. When Daniel, as the interpreter of the Divine message to Belshazzar, named the sin of that monarch which was about to be punished, he did not mention the sins of impurity, drunkenness, or sacrilege, though of all these he had been guilty. He declared the sin which lies at the root of all sins, because it has to do with man's relation to God—"The God in Whose hand thy breath is, and Whose are all thy ways, hast thou not glorified" (Dan. v. 23). In that charge we are reminded of the fact that our very being, in all its powers and possibilities, is of Divine origin.

Paul, preaching to the Athenians on Mars' Hill, makes the same statement, in terms, if possible, more explicit—"In Him we live, and move, and have our being" (Acts xvii. 28). We are the creation of God. Spirit, soul, and body, each in its own possibility; and the one being, resulting from the union, is the result of Divine conception and creation. Every human being is a concrete thought of God. God therefore knows the potentiality of each of us, and the line of our development, and it is only as we are able to discover His Will and obey it, that we shall move along the one to the full realization of the other.

The folly of conditioning conduct by the thoughts or wishes of other human beings is apparent in the light of this fact. To the declaration of John that "No man hath seen God at any time"

(John i. 18), we all agree. Not so readily do we assent to the assertion that no man hath seen man at any time, yet it is equally true. The outward form and tone of voice are familiar, but my essential friend who tabernacles in the body I touch, and conveys his thought through the medium of the speech I hear, I have never yet seen. No man knows perfectly and completely his fellow-man. The mother that bore me, the wife of my heart, the children of my love, do not know me. They are all familiar with the sound of my voice, the touch of my hand, and the fall of my foot on the stair; but all the deeps that lie behind, held for ever sacred from the possibility of intrusion, of these they have no final and complete knowledge.

And yet, forsooth, we are perpetually in danger of taking our law of life from the opinion of some mortal who has no adequate knowledge of the perils and possibilities of our complex nature. Oh, the folly of it! As well let the blacksmith repair our watch, or the collier tune our harp, as allow man, ignorant of the essence and intention of our complex life, to arrange for its conduct. The interference of a human being between another and God is an impertinence and a blasphemy, whatever the name by which the interferer is called, whether it be priest, or teacher, or friend.

Equally foolish is man's attempt to govern himself, for it is equally true that no man has seen himself, neither does any man know himself. The old Greek philosopher said his last and best thing when he said, "Man, know thyself," because he thus brought man face to face with the impossible; and when a man is brought there, he is in the place where it is possible for him to acquaint himself with God and be at peace.

In our younger days we imagine that we know the possibilities of our being, and are able to plan and arrange the whole line of progress. The years are startling revealers. As they pass, we discover new powers for good and evil that had lain dormant within, and of which we had absolutely no consciousness until some crisis aroused and called forth to action the sleeping forces. How we trembled when we found that there was the power of murder lying hidden in our heart! How we suffered when we came to know of a surety that, in spite of all our earlier boasting, we too had the making of the traitor within, and might have kissed the Master to His death!

Ah, those days of time-tables, and

programmes, and pledges, and promises, when we proudly said we were masters of ourselves. Through what disappointments, and agonies, and wounds, some of us have come to our first real knowledge, that we are ignorant of ourselves, and cannot therefore govern ourselves.

This drives us to one conclusion. Our demand for perfection can only be met by our living, and moving, and having our being wholly within the Will of God. Our neighbour's law fails through the limitation of his knowledge. Our own programme collapses because of our ignorance. The Will of God moving within the realm of His perfect knowledge leads us on to perfection, and will at last set us in His presence unafraid.

Procures Pleasure

"'Though he slay me,' I would rest
  In His Sovereign Will,
For the joy to feel His arms
  Wrapped about me still.

"'Though he slay me,' I would sing
  Alleluia lays;
For the Master's slaying-place
  Is the gate of praise.

"'Though He slay me,' I would cry,
  'Lord, our wills are one;
Spare or slay me as Thou wilt;
  Let Thy Will be done!'

"'Though He slay me,' yet in Him
  All my soul would trust,
Not, alone, because it *may*,
  But because it *must!*"

L. A. BENNETT ("Alleluia Songs").

PROCURES PLEASURE

V

MAN'S nature is such that, in addition to perfection, it demands pleasure. How that demand is met in the Will of God may thus be declared:—

> God's Will is perfect, because He is love, and only Love can, and Love can only, make laws for man which will provide him with perfect pleasure.

That is a double proposition. Let us consider it.

I. *Only love can make laws for man which will provide him with perfect pleasure.*—Disinterestedness lies at the heart of all pure love. " Love . . . seeketh not its own." It is almost impossible to discuss the true nature of love from the midst of the limitations of human life as we know it. It is so easy to judge love by the partial realization of it that has come within our consciousness. We love those that love us, those that please us, those that like us; and at the root of all this, in the last analysis, there is but a refined form of selfishness.

The Divine fact of love is infinitely greater than these human imitations. Occasionally it seems to take possession of a human heart, and is then the subject of wonder to all men. Love, however, must ever be judged from its essential being and manifestation in the character of God. There it is wholly unselfish, and consists of perfect affection for an object, without ulterior motive. There only is Shakespeare's description of it fully realized.

> "Love is not love
> Which alters when it alteration finds,
> Or bends with the remover to remove:
> O no! it is an ever-fixèd mark,
> That looks on tempests and is never shaken."

When love becomes the motive of law, then law conditions the true happiness of the one that is loved. To do this, love is never blind, but takes the largest possible outlook, and acts in its government not only for the present moment, but for all the issues of that moment; not only for the final issues, but also for all the present moments that contribute to its making. No other motive for law is equal to meeting the demand for pleasure. Righteousness, apart from its relation to love, may do many cruel things. The doctrine of the survival of the fittest, in its higher aspect, is a protest against unrightness; but it has within itself no remedy for failure, and ruthlessly sweeps away all the weak and fallen. The majesty and dignity of kingship will not ensure the pleasure of the subject in all cases. Law growing from selfishness will, in the nature of things, only bring happiness to those who minister to the self-seeking propensity of the law-giver. No law that my fellow-man can make for me is perfectly to be trusted to ensure my pleasure, because I am never certain of the hidden and yet powerful motive that may give birth to that law. Love only can condition the life of the subject in perfect happiness.

II. *Love can only make laws for man which will provide him with perfect pleasure.*—Its very nature, as we have already seen, makes this a necessity. Herein lies the proof our present proposition. The Will of God ensures the pleasure of man, because God is love. This is, perhaps, at once the simplest and sublimest statement that revelation has made concerning the nature of God. Theologians have spoken of love as an attribute of Deity. Should it not rather be spoken of as the essence of the Divine, of which the attributes are the component parts? As a man's character is the sum and substance of his characteristics, so is the essence of the Divine the sum and substance of Divine attributes. Holiness, justice, beneficence—all these and others lie within the compass of love. To deny either is to deny love. To deny love is to contradict all. If, then, God is love, His Will is the Will of love; and the common mistake that law and love are in any sense antagonistic must be once and for ever abandoned. There is no divergence between the two. Browning sang truly—

> "I report, as a man may, of God's work:
> All's love, but all's law."

In the economy of God, love is law, and law is love.

The twofold denomination of John is not without significance. We speak of him as the Apostle of Love. Jesus called him a Son of Thunder. There is no contradiction in the thoughts. There was never yet an apostle of love who was not also a son of thunder. In the writings of John, the two words most often occurring are the words "commandment" and "love," and there is no contradiction, but rather unity of thought in the fact.

Procures Pleasure

The law of God being then the expression of His love, seeks the perfect happiness of all those who obey it. When Jesus upon the Mount enunciated the ethics of His kingdom, the first word that fell from His lips indicated the purpose of His heart. It was the word "Happy." To make man happy is the purpose of God, and for the realization of that purpose Jesus came to live, to teach, to die. The law He enunciated was the most stringent and exacting that humanity had ever heard, and it was so because love makes no peace with aught that harms, and is the most relentless foe of every foe of the loved one.

Every prohibition of God, and every command He lays upon men, have their reason in His good-will toward men. Nothing is denied to the subjects of His kingdom capriciously, or merely for the satisfaction of some motive outside these subjects. Love prohibits that which, if permitted, would blight the life and mar the pleasure. It is also true that every commandment calling to paths of duty is the outbreathing of love. There are moments when such pathways are rough and thorny and tortuous; but love never sends men along them save when, in the way, something is to be gained which will more than compensate for the suffering, and which can only be gained through the suffering.

> " Every joy or trial
>   Falleth from above,
> Traced upon our dial
>   By the Sun of love."

Man's capacity for pleasure finds its full satisfaction when his life is surrendered to the Will of God. There is first the immediate delight of obedience. The response to love is in itself the essence of delight. This is illustrated from all that we know of love in the human relation, but its highest realization is to be found in this realm of submission to the government of God. Infinite meaning lies within the words of Christ, " I delight to do Thy will, O my God."

Not only is there this joy of love's response to love, there is also the hope of consummation: for if the present will of love be delightful, the perfect issue of love will be the perfection of delight. Consequently, through all the mystery that often surrounds the obedience of to-day, there shines the glow of the perfect consummation which alone can satisfy the Eternal Love.

The heaven towards which we look is, as to our own condition, realized capacity and realized functions of being. The powers which are to-day suggestions, prophecies, will then be possessions; and these all, moving within the realm of the Divine intention, will create the highest delight of which the spirit of man is capable. It is in this sense that the old word of the Psalmist is true: "In Thy presence is fulness of joy; at Thy right hand are pleasures for evermore."

Not, however, to the future merely do we look for this answer to the second demand of our nature. Here and now, to abide in the Will of God is to find the secret of happiness in all life. Submission to the King involves the finding of the mystic key that opens every avenue of pure delight, for in His Will the powers which He in love created are no longer prostituted to ignoble purposes, but serve the purpose of that love creation.

Promises Perpetuity

"Not built with hands is that fair radiant chamber
Of God's untroubled rest,
Where Christ awaits to lay his weary-hearted
In stillness on His breast.

Not built on sands of time or place to perish,
When tempests roar—
But on the mighty Rock of Ages founded,
It stands for evermore—

Not only in the day of distant dawning,
When past are desert years,
But now, amidst the turmoil and the battle,
The mocking and the tears,

That Chamber still and stately waits us ever,
That sacred pure retreat—
That rest in Arms of tenderest enfoldings,
That welcome passing sweet.

O Home of God, my Father's joy and gladness,
O riven Veil, whereby I enter in!
There can my soul forget the grave, the weeping,
The weariness and sin.

O Chamber, all thine agate windows opened
To face the radiant east—
O holy Temple, where the saints are singing,
Where Jesus is the Priest—

Illumined with the everlasting glory,
Still with the peace of God's eternal Now,
Thou, God, my Rest, my Refuge, and my Tower—
My Home art Thou."

T. S. M.

("Hymns of Ter Steegen and others").

PROMISES PERPETUITY

VI

THE third demand of man is for perpetuity. That also is secured by those who dwell wholly within the Will of God.

The argument may be simply stated thus:—

> God's Will is perfect, because He *is*, and the Eternal alone can make laws which include the past, present, and future, so as to secure perpetuity.

Nothing is more restful to the heart of man than the sense of the eternity of God. The thought is utterly beyond our perfect comprehension, for the mind of man cannot grasp the thought of eternity. The very fact, however, of our inability to do so is the reason of the security we feel when we remember that God is Himself eternal. The secrets of the past, all unknown to us, are ever present to His omniscient mind. Upon the mystery of the future the light of His perfect knowledge rests; and the problems of to-day that fret and trouble us are seen by Him in their relation to the past and to the future, and for that reason cease to be to Him perplexing, as they are to us.

In the eternity of God, time has but one significance, it is perpetually and unceasingly "Now." The name by which He revealed Himself to Moses at the burning bush is full of significance. He is the "I AM." Combining this fact with those considered in previous chapters, of His Creatorship and His love, we argue at once that the laws He makes for the creatures of His hand and the children of His love, are laws that will take in the sum of things, and so condition the present, that it shall hold within it the power and the promise of the future.

Every present law of God for man is based upon the fact of the past, and moves towards the purpose of the future. What He wills for each person to-day takes into account all the forces and facts of the past. Previous failings in the individual life; tendencies inherited from the generations that have gone; the accumulated forces that propel men from the dead centuries—are all present to the mind of God, when He arranges the programme of individual lives.

So also the future is known to Him. The true line of life's development, with all the lines that cross and thwart it. Words that we often have to make use of are never required in the vocabulary of God. We speak of contingency, exigency, accident. He cannot be surprised. Nothing happens, in the sense in which we use that word. He marks the approach of every foe, knows whence it comes, sets the limit of its opposition; saying ever to Satan, as He said in the case of Job, "So far mayest thou go; only here and there thou shalt stay thy hand."

It follows, necessarily, that where life is governed only within the Will of God, every date and every event become links in the chain of a perfect whole. All contribute to a finality. It is impossible here and now for us to discover the relation of the present moment either to past or to future. But that relation is always present to the mind of God. We are permitted occasional gleams of light upon this truth as the years of our life pass on. The light falls in the act of retrospection. Looking back to-day to the events of years that have passed, we begin to discover their meaning. They are seen to be part of the Divine mosaic. The keen disappointment, the whelming sorrow, came after all as a necessity out of the past, and hold within themselves the elements that make the present, and colour all the future. The present place of service and of blessing could not have been but for the events that seemed to create confusion.

From this distance we see how God was moving in the infinite order of His ceaseless love, and what we thought confusion was but the sign of His progress. What light is flung upon the pathway of each day if once this fact is understood. The day is not done with when its sun sets. The deeds of any given hour are not fully comprehended in the passing of its sixty minutes. If the deeds of the days have been those planned by God, then they are days, the full blossoming of which will be found in the perfect light of the everlasting day. It has been said that every flower that decks the sod has its root far back in eternity. So also every human life, in the Will and purpose of God, is linked to the past and to the future, and His laws for it forget no fact of all the ages.

Need anything further be written to prove the wisdom of abandoning life to His Will? See how all other laws fail when placed in comparison with this. The best-loved friend I have cannot compass within the facts of certain knowledge the events of the next hour. They may advise, but their advice is necessarily tentative. They would go this way if—and how much depends upon the *if*. A thousand chances may prove the folly of their wisdom, the shortsightedness of their policy.

This is never so with the soul that has no law save that of the Divine Will.

> " He always wins who sides with God,
> To him no chance is lost."

The same criticism will apply to self-made programmes. One might, perchance, make a programme for one's own life for a week if one knew all that could possibly happen within that week. Seeing, however, that that knowledge does not extend to the next minute, the folly of a self-governed life becomes apparent. Of course it is necessary that we should have our programme and our plan and our arrangement, but the more necessary thing is that all such should be prefaced by the old-fashioned and almost obsolete letters *D.V.* "If the Lord will, we shall both live, and do this or that. . . . To him therefore that knoweth to do good, and doeth it not, to him it is sin." Thus James states the true attitude of man towards his future and his God. If our plans are made with this reservation, how often we shall have to thank God for their spoiling; how perpetually has He broken up our programme in order that His Will should be done, and how true we have found it to be that—

> "God's Will is sweetest to us when
> It triumphs at our cost."

The restfulness and peace of this attitude of surrender to the Divine Will lies in the fact that the Eternal God, Who in infinite love has created us, has done so for eternal comradeship with Himself; and if He govern the life, He will bring it, notwithstanding all the forces that seem to be against it, to the place of full and undying existence. There is no other law of life that will secure this. "The world passeth away, and the lust thereof, but he that doeth the Will of God abideth for ever." From the centre of that Will man may look out upon change and decay, upon death and destruction, and know that he is perfectly safe from them all; yea, master of every one.

> "Things that once were wild alarms
>   Cannot now disturb my rest;
> Closed in everlasting arms,
>   Pillowed on the loving breast.
> Oh to lie for ever here,
>   Doubt and care and self resign,
> While He whispers in my ear—
>   I am His, and He is mine!

God's Perfect Will

" His for ever, only His,
  Who the Lord and me shall part;
Ah, with what a rest of bliss
  Christ can fill the loving heart!
Heaven and earth may fade and flee,
  First-born light in gloom decline,
But while God and I shall be,
  I am His and He is mine."

Practicable Because of Its Nature

"Thus is Christianity concerned, not with merely a section of life—with the 'affairs of the soul'—but with all of it. No life—as I think Luther has said somewhere—is more worldly than a Christian's. It embraces everything that makes us what we are—all that, lived in a certain light and treated from a certain point of view. One of the great wrongs that ecclesiastical Christianity has done religion is to disparage or deny this, to give us the impression that a Christian life lived in the cloister is higher and holier than one lived in the family, the market, the secular arena of the world, and to bid us look to types of the former rather than the latter for saintship. I cannot find any meaning such as this in the fact of Christ. The carpenter of Nazareth, who was among men 'eating and drinking'—He is 'our only Saint.' We must secularize saintship by sanctifying the secular life."—P. CARNEGIE SIMPSON ("The Fact of Christ").

PRACTICABLE BECAUSE OF ITS NATURE

VII

For the reasons as stated, we grant that the Will of God should be the best law of life for man. Having granted so much, a new question immediately arises: Is the doing of the Will possible to man? An ideal that cannot be realized may be a vision of beauty, but it lacks the essential element that creates the true ideal—that, namely, of practicability. Men do not climb after the inaccessible. Men make no effort to mount to the moon. Grant the accessibility, and distance becomes an incentive to climbing. The Will of God is practicable for three reasons:—

1. Because of its nature.
2. Because it is revealed.
3. Because of supernatural power, communicated to those who will to do it.

We proceed to deal with these three statements in these three chapters.

The Will of God includes and conditions all that God has created. Doing the Will of God does not consist in the development of the spiritual side of man's nature, at the expense of the other sides. The apostle prayed for the Thessalonian Christians, that their "spirit and soul and body" might "be preserved entire, without blame, at the coming of our Lord Jesus Christ."

We are suffering from the art of the Old Masters. They gave men a wrong conception of God and of sainthood.

Take, for instance, what Ruskin speaks of as "that infinite monstrosity and hypocrisy, Raphael's cartoon of the charge to Peter." Let me give you an analysis of his criticism on the picture:—

(1) Twelve apostles, when only seven were present.

(2) Curled hair and sandals, after a night in sea mists.

(3) Dresses with trains—an apostolic fishing costume.

(4) No fire of coals, but an Italian landscape with villas and churches.

(5) The apostles not round Christ, but in a line to be shown.

That is a fair sample of the conception of sainthood which the Old Masters gave the world. They lifted men and women out of the ordinary experiences of human life, and put them upon impossible planes. This was due to a misconception of the Will of God. These Old Masters did not understand that God does not call men away from the commonplaces of the busy days, but conditions their life within them, until the meanest thing flashes and gleams with the glory of the heavens.

Another illustration is that offered by Monasticism. The monastic system was the outcome of a pure and holy desire, but it was based upon a misconception of God. Men desired to serve their age by prayer; and to do so, retired from the hurry and rush of life, turning their back upon marriage, parenthood, home, and friendship. It was a fatal mistake. When men retire from the conflict to pray, they cut the nerves of prayer. Men only pray with prevailing power, who do so amid the sobs and sighing of the race.

PRACTICABLE BECAUSE REVEALED

VIII

WHILE the fact that the Will of God includes and conditions all His creation is a most blessed one, yet it is not sufficient to prove its practicability. One person may be deeply interested in the history of another, but this fact is of little practical use to the one in whom this interest is taken, unless it is made known. I may have plans which are the very best possible for my children, but the first conditions of their being carried into effect by these children is that I should make them known to them. In the very nature of the case, the Will of God for every human life must be the best; and because of His intimate acquaintance with, and interest in, every part of the being He has created, it must be possible to do that Will if it can be known.

That this Will may be discovered by every human being is the distinct claim of Christianity. The central verity of Christianity is Christ, and He is the revelation in a Person of God's Will for man. Moreover, the perpetual method of God with man is that of revealing to him immediately the Divine intention and purpose concerning him. We say, therefore, that the Will of God is practicable because it is revealed.

In the life of Jesus there was a perfect unfolding of the thought that was in the heart of God when He said "Let Us make man in Our image" (Gen. i. 26). He was indeed the "image of the invisible God" (Col. i. 15); "the very image of His substance" (Heb. i. 3). "The Word became flesh, and dwelt among us (and we beheld His glory, the glory as of the only begotten from the Father), full of grace and truth" (John i. 14). This is John's testimony concerning Him. It is a sad commentary upon the blindness of the human heart through sin, that the vast mass of the people who came into contact with Him during the years of His sojourn upon the earth, saw no beauty in Him that they should desire Him. Through the process of the centuries, and by the teaching of the Spirit, men are coming to understand the wonderful glory and beauty of His Person and character, and are now recognizing that all perfection of life, individually, socially, religiously, finds in Him its first and chief expression.

Individually, He yielded Himself

wholly to the claim of God, and then faced life's duties and responsibilities with a courage and devotion that transmuted the common things of the passing days into service so sacred, that it contributed to the final glories of the ages to come. He toiled upon the earth as a man, interested in the flowers of the field, and the birds of the air, and the children of the street. Gentle and strong, trusted of the weakest, feared of all tyrants, He moved without strife of words, or lifting up the voice in self-advertisement, through the Divinely marked programme of the waiting years, to the cross of ultimate pain, which He made the centre and source of all healing for wounded and broken humanity. He was the supreme illustration of the possibilities of individual life conditioned ever and only in the Will of God.

In all social relationships His action was such as to reveal God's Will in an entirely new light to men, thus revolutionizing human thought and human society. Without staying for a single illustration, let the mind dwell for one moment on His unvarying attitude towards women; and then remember how, since the years of His human life, woman the world over has lived in a new realm, for the day of her final emancipation dawned with His appearing. His obedience to government was exhibited in the paying of taxes, and was startlingly proved by the fact that when they would encompass His Death, His enemies had to fall back upon a religious charge, having no civil one to prefer against Him. His attitude of tenderness towards all sinners incurred the condemnation of the religious enthusiasts of His day, who had so misread the heart of God as to imagine that love was for the good, and nothing but stern anger and vindictiveness for the fallen.

Religiously He gave us a radiant revelation of the truth so hard for men to learn, that religion is not an addendum to life, but is life itself. With Him God was first; and there was no second. The critics of the ages may be challenged to discover a single action of His life as chronicled that was not true to the keyword of that life, " I must be about My Father's business."

In that perfect life God revealed His Will for every human being. It was not the life of an angel visitor. Its glory lay in the fact of its humanness, and that fact brings it within the realm of the possible to every son and daughter of the human race.

Not only once in a person has the Will been revealed; it is perpetually and immediately revealed to all such as desire to know it. The work of the Holy Spirit is ever that of indicating to man the intention and purpose of God for him.

This may be stated in another way. The Holy Spirit is to "take of the things of Christ and reveal them to men;" and this is infinitely more than explaining the doctrines concerning Him. It is the showing to individual souls of the way in which, under all the circumstance of life, Christ would think, or act, or speak. Jesus was, and is, the "Light that lighteth every man that cometh into the world," and thus He is perpetually the revelation of the Divine Will to men.

It does not necessarily follow that when the light falls upon the spirit of man, he understands the source of the light. The light is the first fact; the understanding of the source follows. The little child may play with the golden sunshine, and yet have no knowledge of the sun. That will come in the process of the years. Let any person, if it be possible, go back in life to that moment when the conscience first detected the difference between right and wrong. That shining of the light of right was the outshining of the glory of Christ's perfection upon the spirit, and the consequent revelation of the Will of God.

All this was not then understood, but enough was understood to make man responsible. If in that moment the right was chosen, Christ was obeyed, and the Will of God was done. If the wrong was chosen, the light was insulted, and the government of God rebelled against.

Thus God does reveal His Will to man, and man chooses between obedience and disobedience. The measure and clearness of personal revelation depends upon this act of man. To obedient souls the light becomes perpetually brighter, for he "that doeth the Will shall know of the teaching." To those who disobey, the light dies away, until they stumble in darkness upon the mountains, and imagine God does not reveal His Will to man; whereas the truth is, that having "loved the darkness rather than the light," they have become blind.

To the soul new-born the will of God is revealed again, not as a perfect and final programme of life, but in a claim demanding immediate obedience, and then by successive revelations concerning the pathway of life. So that a man may say, as he steps out upon his new life,

> "One step I see before me,
> 'Tis all I need to see."

When Saul of Tarsus was apprehended of Jesus Christ, he was not told that he was to become the apostle to the Gentiles, the mightiest missionary of the Cross, the greatest theologian of the Church. Jesus said to him, "Rise, enter into the city, and it shall be told thee what thou must do." The next step was marked. Taking this, another was revealed; and so ever on, until at last, saying, "I have fought a good fight; I have finished my course; I have kept the faith"—he passed to the place of perfect light and perfect life.

PRACTICABLE BY NEW LIFE

IX

In writing to the Philippians, Paul says, "For it is God which worketh in you both to will and to work, for His good pleasure" (ii. 13). This statement occurs between two injunctions. The first has reference to personal salvation, and the second declares the duty of man in relation to the world. The first reads, "Work out your own salvation with fear and trembling"; and the second, "Do all things without murmurings and disputings; that ye may be blameless and harmless, children of God without blemish, in the midst of a crooked and perverse generation, among whom ye are seen as lights in the world." The declaration referred to brings both the positive and relative statements within the realm of practical possibility, "For it is God which worketh in you." This Divine inworking makes the human outworking easy, and simple, and delightful. For every demand made upon us as Christian men and women, there is sufficient, overwhelming supply in the communication of Divine energy.

"God worketh *in* you." This implies the actual presence of God at the centre of our being. The very simplicity of these words renders them difficult of understanding; for no man understands the complex and marvellous mechanism of his own personality. God worketh *in* you—not outside, but in—in the place where thought is born, and the throne of the will is set up, and the affections have their seat; in the inward shrine of the being God worketh.

Put emphasis now on another word. " God *worketh* in you." He is there, not merely holding possession while we work, but also to

> " Direct, control, suggest each day,
> All we design, or do, or say;
> That all our powers, with all their might,
> In His sole glory may unite."

" God worketh in you." The value of this statement may be learned by inserting another word in place of " in." " For it is God which worketh *for* you." By this alteration the message is robbed of its power in a moment. To work *for* us, may be to work apart from us, without consultation with us. This is suggestive of duality, which is not always necessarily a harmony.

Try another preposition. " It is God

which worketh *with* you." That would indicate some one by the side of us, willing, when the burden becomes too heavy, to help to bear it; willing when the pathway becomes difficult, to come into consultation. This also is suggestive of dual personality, and perchance conflict.

"God which worketh *in* you" implies perfect union. God *in* you, creating desire, energizing the will, so that the will becomes, not merely as a poetical sentiment, but as a glorious fact, the Will of God. That is, indeed, the supreme glory of the Christian position—"it is God which worketh," not "for" merely; not "with" only; but "it is God which worketh *in* you."

"It is God which worketh *in* you both *to will* and *to do*." Two facts are here stated which are yet one, for willing and doing are always united. "To will"—

that touches the inner life, the springs of action; "to do"—that touches the outer life, the streams of action.

Think first of the inner, "to will." This word has within it the thought of active determination of what is to be done. Not determination apart from ourselves, but God in us, taking hold of our wills, creating our desires—sometimes through indirect agencies—giving us desire in a certain direction, affecting and moulding our wills, drawing them into the avenues of true action, by His own indwelling. "It is God which worketh in you *to will*." If this be true, then the will, so created, must necessarily result in the harmony of our wills with His own.

The work of God does not end here. "It is God which worketh in you to will and *to do*." As the thought of the inworking God, *willing,* touches the springs of action, so necessarily the thought of God *doing* touches the streams of action. "It is God which worketh in you to will and to work." It might truthfully be translated "to effectually work." The suggestion is not of the doing that fails, but of the doing that succeeds: not of the effort that tries, but of the effort which triumphs.

This union of the purified will, and the energized life, is equal to the accomplishment of the double purpose: "Work out your own salvation," and "be blameless and harmless . . . in the midst of a crooked and perverse generation, among whom ye shine as lights in the world." The poor, weak, paralysed, sin-smitten soul rises into the dignity of a new life, confronts the future with hope, faces his enemies with defiance, and says: "I can do all things in Him that strengtheneth me. I will work out my own salvation: I will live the life which is blameless, harmless, without rebuke, because it is God which worketh in me to will and to do."

What will be the result? "His good pleasure;" that which gives His heart satisfaction. If we shrink from that, we shrink from all the blessedness within the thought. "His good pleasure," the thing that pleases Him. Go back to the story of creation. When God had made the earth, and put man upon it, "God saw everything that He had made, and, behold, it was very good"—God's good pleasure. God was pleased with His own work; found delight in its perfection.

There came a day when God could say this no more—a day when sin had entered. The sigh and sob of humanity began amid the trees of the garden of God, and the great surging sorrow of the race was born amid the hills of perfection. From then onward the heart of God was not at rest until, long, weary, and yet necessary centuries having passed, there came " the second Adam, the Lord from heaven, the quickening Spirit."

If we would know the good pleasure of God, man must be seen in all his perfection. In Christ we have the revelation of perfect manhood. Think of His perfection of tenderness, His beauty of character, of all the great overwhelming strength which centred in His sacred Person. In beholding Him, behold the " good pleasure of God." " It is God which worketh in you both to will and to do of His good pleasure."

To make us what Jesus was, God

works within us; and until that is finally accomplished, the heart of God will never be at rest concerning us: not until that moment dawns, which must come for all who put their trust in Him, when the perfect Son of the living God shall present the many sons whom He brings to glory, in the presence of His glory, without blemish in exceeding joy. That is the intended issue; that is the consummation; that is the crowning and the joy.

This view of life contained within vital Christianity is a declaration of our possibilities. We are equal to this, because God is equal to it. We have nothing which we have not received; but we have received something in our creation which makes us equal to that. Before any being can reach the altitude of true success, there must be within that being the possibility of reaching the altitude. We are made in the image of the invisible God, with the stamp of Divine possession upon us. Shall we not swing the heart's door widely open that He may come in, to work in us " both to will and to work, for His good pleasure "?

The Ultimate Realization

"'Twill all be right
At last:
When weary night
Is past,
When light shall dawn
And cometh morn
Upon that peaceful shore,
Where storm and cloud no more
Oppress the soul.

"'Twill all be shown
Some day;
Each step unknown
Of way
By which Christ led
Where feet oft bled.
Where fell the bitter tear.
As sorrow's doubt and fear
So oft made sad.

"Then shall we see
His throne;
Then shall we be
His own:
When endeth night
And dawneth light.
That day of days so dear
May even now be near,
We watch and pray.

"Dear heart, why sad?
Christ comes.
Dear heart, be glad;
Christ comes.
The hour draws nigh
Of midnight cry.
Then ends our brief life-pain,
Then comes eternal gain,
Where reigns our King."

E. G. WELLESLEY-WESLEY.
("Songs of the Heart").

THE ULTIMATE REALIZATION

X

So far we have considered the subject of the Word of God within the compass of probationary life. The perfection possible to-day is that of condition which ensures progress; and the possibility of progress ever speaks of something not yet attained. The supreme consciousness of those who to-day are most certainly living within the Will of God is that of incompleteness. All is partial, limited. By comparison with the exceeding worth and beauty of our Lord, we feel that our worship is almost worthless, and we are constantly constrained to say that,

> "Hosannas languish on our tongues,
> And our devotion dies."

And when we have done the fullest day's work possible to us, having, so far as we know, filled the hours with sacrificial service, we yet have to say, "At best we are unprofitable servants." When we have walked in the Will as revealed to us for the present moment, we are always conscious that His ultimate Will is so much better than any present realization. This sense of shortcoming is in itself an incentive to diligence. It is because we have "not yet apprehended" . . . that "forgetting the things which are behind," we "press on toward the goal." This pushing towards the goal, however, does not mark dissatisfaction with the discipline of the pathway. Abiding in the Will of God, we recognize that all the circumstances of life are necessary for our perfecting, and are overruled by Infinite Love.

The Ultimate Realization

" Stayed upon Jehovah,
Hearts are fully blest,
Finding as He promised,
Perfect peace and rest."

The questions yet will arise, What is to be the issue? whither does the pathway tend? It is with this subject that the present chapter deals, not exhaustively, but by suggestion.

Much has been written on the future condition of the saints. Richard Baxter wrote a treatise, in four parts and forty-six chapters, full of thought and beauty; and many others have contributed to the valuable literature. Our thought in this chapter is to be confined to the subject of the doing of the Will of God; and there are four facts recorded in the New Testament which are illuminative of the subject.

I. *Unclouded Vision.*

Paul says, "For now we see in a mirror darkly; but then face to face" (1 Cor. xiii. 12); and John declares, "We shall see Him even as He is" (1 John iii. 2). After faith has had its perfect work, it will be swallowed up in sight. To-day we love, not having seen. Conscious of His presence, apprehending in some measure His love and beauty, we walk by faith amid the mists and mysteries, or underneath the blue, which is also the limitation of vision.

"Soon the whole,
Like a parchèd scroll,
Shall before my amazèd sight uproll;
And, without a screen,
At one burst be seen
The Presence wherein I have ever been."

II. *Perfect Correspondence.*

The first result of this, according to John, will be that of perfect correspondence with our Master. "We shall be like Him" (1 John iii. 2). In the moment of vision, the word of the Master on the Mount of Beatitudes—whether that word was promise or command, or both—will be fulfilled in our experience; "ye shall be perfect, even as your heavenly Father is perfect." All the possibilities of our being will be fulfilled. Everything that was in the thought of God for us, as to capacity, will be realized, and we shall thus be prepared to fulfil the highest functions of our life.

As to-day it is true that where there is no vision, the people perish; and the constant cry of the human heart is that of Philip, "Show us the Father, and it sufficeth us"; and the immediate consciousness of the soul that has even the partial vision of God, seeing through a glass darkly, is that of healing; so at last the full and unclouded vision will be final salvation, perfect healing, and absolute satisfaction. Nay, does not the thought of the apostle overtake and run ahead of all these thoughts, glorious as they are. "We shall be like Him." Nothing can be added to this. It defies analysis. If an uninspired statement, it is the most daring blasphemy of the mind of man. If the word is Spirit-taught, it is the most gracious unveiling of the infinite love of God. Like Him, and therefore fitted for fellowship of thought and action; like Him, and so falling into line with all His mighty movements through the unexplored spaces and the unborn ages.

III. *Full Knowledge.*

Paul speaks of another result accruing from unclouded vision. "Now I know in part; but then shall I know even as also I have been known" (1 Cor. xiii. 12). The messages of the Spirit to the Church, delivered through human agents, are all messages which met the need of the writer, and so appeal to thousands of similar temperaments. The Spirit's declaration of correspondence through John answers the question of spiritual devotion. The Spirit's message of full knowledge through Paul answers the problem of mental activity. Through all the system of Paul's writing his mind is discovered active, alert, mighty, pressing on, desiring to know. He thinks of the Spirit as "knowing the deep things of God." His perpetual prayer for his children in the faith is that they may have full knowledge of God; and here, after describing in language that seems as though it might be a part of the poetry of heaven, the nature and the activity of love, his active mind reasserts itself, and he seems to lift his eyes and gaze away to the land of light, and exult in the consciousness that " Then I shall know even as also I have been known." Thus we learn that the condition of heaven will be that of perfect light. The problems that vex us to-day; the perpetually recurring mysteries that demand repeated acts of faith—these will all find their answer, not so much in the process of teaching or revealing, but in the vision of the Master Himself. Seeing, we shall know. Seeing face to face, we shall know even as we are known.

IV. *Unceasing Service.*

Out of these grows the fourth glorious fact, that of unceasing service. " They serve Him day and night in His temple "

(Rev. vii. 15). "His servants shall do Him service; and they shall see His face" (Rev. xxii. 3, 4). It is not within the purpose of this volume to discuss the nature of the service. The fact is enough. We shall see Him, and want to serve. We shall be like Him, and be able to serve. We shall know, and be prepared to serve. Inspiration for service in vision; equipment for service in correspondence; preparation for service in knowledge! Thus Himself will be the reason of all the service of the new life, and therefore His Will will be the plane of heaven's activity.

> "Then we shall be where we would be;
> Then we shall be what we should be;
> Things which are not now, nor could be,
> Then shall be our own."

The last words of the fourth book of the Psalms declare the call of God to men, "Let all the people say, Amen; Hallelujah" (Psa. cvi. 48, R. V., *marg.*). Let there be acquiescence in the Divine Will, followed by a note of praise. This is the order of faith's activity—first, Amen; and then in faith, Hallelujah. Praise grows out of obedience and submission; resolute obedience in the power of faith is ever preparing for the song. There is nothing better in this world, no higher experience, than that we should, to every revelation of the Will of God, utter our whole-hearted Amen, and crown it with our joyous Hallelujah.

But presently, in the light of the unclouded vision; in the power of a perfect correspondence to the likeness of our Lord; in the light of full knowledge, and in the gladness of unceasing service—we shall reverse the order of these great words. "After these things I heard as it were a great voice of a great multitude in heaven, saying, Hallelujah. And a second time they say, Hallelujah. . . . And the four and twenty elders and the four living creatures fell down and worshipped God that sitteth on the throne, saying, Amen; Hallelujah . . . And I heard as it were the voice of a great multitude, and as the voice of many waters, and as the voice of mighty thunders, saying, Hallelujah" (Rev. xix. 1-6). Here first the song, and then the submission, and yet again the song. It is that vision of the perfect consummation that inspires the song.

At last all opposing forces are overcome, and the kingdom of the heavens is realized through all the vast realms over which it is God's right to reign.

At last the prayer taught by Christ is answered, the Name is hallowed, the kingdom come, the Will is done, and the unending Hallelujah follows the unlimited Amen.

Then begins the absolutely perfect service of which all the imperfect service of these probationary days is the hardly articulate prophecy. Then life moves unchecked, unhindered, toward highest forms of expression and most glorious inter-relation, because it is absolutely homed in the Will of God.

Bear me on Thy rapid wing,
  Everlasting Spirit!
Where bright choirs of angels sing,
  And Thy saints inherit;
Waiting round the Eternal throne,
Joys immortal are their own:
This the cry of every one—
'Glory to the Incarnate Son!'

Four and twenty elders rise
  From their princely station,
Shout His glorious victories—
  Sing His great salvation,

The Ultimate Realization

Cast their crowns before the throne,
Cry, in reverential tone,
'Holy, Holy, Holy One,
Glory be to God alone!'

Hark! the thrilling symphonies
  Seem within to seize us;
Add we to their holy lays—
  Jesus, Jesus, Jesus!
Sweetest note in angels' song,
Sweetest sound on mortal tongue,
Sweetest anthem ever known,
Jesus, Jesus reigns alone."

Epilogue

"God, Who once at Pentecost
Sentest down the Holy Ghost:
  Grant us by that Spirit's light,
  Evermore a judgment right;
Through the Son, Who reigns with Thee
In that Spirit's unity.

"God, Who by Thy Spirit taught
Humble souls that asked and sought:
  Grant that He to us may bring
  All His holy comforting;
Through the Son, Who reigns with Thee
In that Spirit's unity.

"God, Whose Spirit came to guide
Faithful people to Thy side:
  Let Him lead us to that shore,
  Whither Christ is gone before;
Through the Son, Who reigns with Thee
In that Spirit's unity."

ELLEN THORNEYCROFT FOWLER.
("A Whitsuntide Hymn").

EPILOGUE

ALL life's urgency is concentrated on the present moment. To-day is all that we possess. Yesterday has passed from us. To-morrow is not ours. God's time for His people is indicated by the two words "now" and "to-day." Our study, therefore, of the subject of the Will of God is of practical and immediate importance in its bearing on the interests of the present. If we remember "all the way which the Lord our God hath led us," it is only in order that, taking warning from our failures, and deriving encouragement from the unfailing faithfulness of God, we may "forget the things that are behind" in our devotion to present duty. If we contemplate the coming glory, it is only that its light may be a source of inspiration to us as we "run with patience the race that is set before us." The Will of God is the supreme subject in every life. The Old and New Testaments alike testify to its importance. Within that Will man finds perfection, pleasure, permanence. It is practicable because of its nature, its revelation, and the fact of its being accompanied with the gift of life, which makes it possible to obey. It is glorious, indeed, for heaven itself lies within the compass of its thought. There remains one subject of immediate practical moment. How may we know the Will of God for to-day, in all the details of the hours as they come and go; and how may we discover it in any crises that may arise?

Two preliminary conditions must be fulfilled, those, namely, of desire and devotion. The desire must amount to readiness to obey. The devotion must be of that practical nature that seeks to know and at all cost follows to do. These conditions being fulfilled, light may be expected in three ways:

From the Word of God.

From the immediate illumination of the indwelling Spirit.

From the combination of circumstances.

Let us examine these separately, and then in their inter-relation.

I. *The Three Indications.*

(1) *The Word of God.*—For the most part, the Bible does not lay down rules of human conduct; it enunciates principles. There are exceptions to be found, arising out of some local circumstances that demanded clear and explicit state-

ment of duty. But as the Bible is a Book for all time and habits and manners change, the framing of rules, which must necessarily change with change of local conditions, would have defeated the high end in view. The enunciation of principles, on the other hand, which never change with changing circumstances, calls forth on the part of man, in every successive generation, his reasoning and reflective powers, and answers the purpose of righteousness.

In coming to the Word of God, therefore, for understanding of the Will of God, we are not to search for texts to defend private judgments. Nor are we, on the other hand, to play tricks with the Bible, in order to discover accidental messages to help us in forming judgments. We are regularly, and devotionally, and intelligently, to study, in order that we may discover the revelation of principles. Where this is done as a habit of the life, the mind will act under the power of these principles, and the conclusions arrived at will be in harmony with the intention of God.

(2) *The Illumination of the Spirit.*—The doctrine of the inner light is not sufficiently taught. To the individual believer, who is, by the very fact of relationship to Christ, indwelt by the Holy Spirit of God, there is granted the direct impression of the Spirit of God on the spirit of man, imparting the knowledge of His Will in matters of the smallest and greatest importance. This has to be sought and waited for. It is at this point that it may be well for the seeker to take counsel with some fellow-Christian, who in prayer and conversation may be enabled to thrown light upon the problem.

It should, however, be remembered that others can only give testimony as to their view of the problem suggested. Such testimony is of great value. It cannot, however, be final, and should only be given as contributing thought, which may aid in solution. No Spirit-taught man or woman will pretend to be able to decide for a second person. Each must at last, having received help, it may be, from conference with other Christians, pass into some place of utter loneliness, where only the voice of the Spirit is heard. To such waiting, a clear and definite answer must come.

(3) *The Combination of Circumstances.*—In the fact of the Divine government, this may be spoken of as the opening and shutting of doors. There is no room for doubt that God does, in infinite wisdom and power, manipulate the

facts and details of all human lives, in such a way as to make "all things work together for good to them that love God." The open door does not necessarily mean the easy pathway. This is a common mistake. One has often heard persons say the way is made plain, and by "plain" they mean easy. And yet, those who know most of the immediate government of God, will confess that the most plain pathway has often been the most difficult.

The open door is an opportunity created, which is in harmony with the principles of the Divine government as declared in Scripture, and the desire for which has been created in that fellowship with God into which no other interest has been allowed to enter. This is a most solemn consideration, and needs the severest caution. There is no realm of human life into which the enemy more successfully passes, and in which he works more destruction, than that of motive. Desires based upon motives other than the highest will often discover open doors which are quite other than those which God would open.

II. *The Threefold Indication.*

The value of the three indications dealt with, lies in the fact that not in any one of them is to be discovered the warrant for action, but in their combination.

(1) With regard to the Word of God, many principles of action therein recognized are not meant for all men at all times. There must also be the inner light and the open door.

(2) With regard to the leading of the Spirit, it cannot be too constantly reaffirmed that such leading is never con-

tradictory to the truth of Scripture. There is so much idle talk to-day about the leading of the Lord, that at this point one would desire to speak most strongly and solemnly. Some awful instances of gross immorality have resulted from people following what they imagined to be the guidance of the Holy Spirit, even though the action was in direct disobedience to the most emphatic statements and requirements of the law of God. This is blasphemy of the worst kind. Whenever, therefore, it is supposed that the Spirit is leading, it is of the gravest importance that such leading should be tested by the principles of the Word.

And again, the Spirit never leads without opening the doors sooner or later. There may have been the waiting of long discipline—and abiding in the Will of God means rejoicing in all such discipline—and patient waiting for His opening of the door, even when the light is clearly shining as to the Spirit's ultimate intention.

(3) The open door that necessitates departure from Scriptural teaching is the work of the devil; and no matter how remarkable the success that appears to follow efforts ostensibly made in the interests of the kingdom of God, if the base of operation is not loyalty to the revealed Will of God in Holy Scripture, the fabric erected is but "hay, wood, stubble," to be destroyed in the cleansing fire at last.

And yet again, the open door, in harmony with the principles of Scripture, is not to be entered, save as a personal call is heard, and one is able to say, I do this because I have the witness of God's Spirit with my spirit that He so wills it.

Thus to summarize. We have ever the

threefold test, which is invaluable as to everyday details, and in the crises of life; the truth of God, contained in the Word of God; the purpose of God indicated by the Spirit of God; the government of God exhibited in the opening of doors by God.

One perpetual condition remains, that of obedience. This word, it will be seen, is not here lightly used. It presupposes a desire to know and to do, expressing itself in devotion to seek and to obey. Such obedience will ever be based on the perfect confidence of the spirit of man in the grace of the Lord Jesus Christ, the love of God, and the communion of the Holy Spirit. Where this confidence exists, the obedience will be unquestioning, immediate, complete.

The tendency of the age is to softness. Some may read this final message, and turning from it say, This is not easy.

Easy! When did Christ suggest ease to men in the method of their own making? Did He not solemnly warn those who would follow Him to count the cost, and indicate that the pathway of His footprints necessitated the denial of self and the taking of the Cross? If the perfection of character, and pleasure of life, and permanence of being for which we profess to be desirous, are ever to be realized, it will be by strenuous action; time, thought, energy, are all necessary.

Let the end be as the beginning. There is but one thing that matters. It is that God's Will should be done. To that end let every one cast sloth away, and, "girding up the loins of the mind, be sober and set the hope perfectly on the grace that is to be brought unto you at the revelation of Jesus Christ." The ultimate issue will be perfect compensation for all the toil of the pathway that leads thereto.